this journal belongs to:

_____

one word to describe myself:

_____

Special thanks to:

Jackie Sullivan, Wellbeing Coordinator at Mosman Public School, Australia and the class of 2S; may your inner exploration continue.

~

Dr Nicky Hirst, Programme Leader/Head of BA (hons) Early Childhood Studies; School of Education, Liverpool John Moores University, UK; for your expert advice.

~

Matt Lynch and Tod Spedding from The International School of Amsterdam, The Netherlands; thank you for helping me discover the sweet taste of self-exploration.

~

My Family, for your continued support and love.

Published by My Wellbeing School 2020
Text and illustrations copyright H. J. Ray
ISBN: 978-0-6488455-5-3

For my Grandma Mary, (1922-1999)

I wish this was taught when you went to school.

Written and illustrated by H. J. Ray

My
Wellbeing
Universe

Contents

~

Author's Note

I began writing My Wellbeing Universe in October 2019, piloting the project for a public school in Sydney, Australia. The project gained impetus when I was asked to talk at the Liverpool John Moores University School of Education conference on wellbeing in primary education. Things were evolving organically, until...

2020.
WE ALL KNOW HOW THAT WENT DOWN.

Here in Australia, it started with the bush fires, then the floods, then the frenzy of toilet paper buying and you know the rest.

Suddenly, My Wellbeing Universe became front and centre of my life, whilst trying to home school my two boisterous boys. I realised the utter necessity of bringing this work into the classroom and at home, NOW. So I skipped the traditional publishing route to fast track this resource and bring it to you sooner rather than later.

The 'old world' we left behind in 2019 is gone. As we collectively look out on this unfamiliar terrain, I am reminded of Joseph Campbell's work on mythology and the hero's journey. "We must be willing to get rid of the life we've planned, so as to have the life that is waiting for us." (Campbell, 1983) Very often it's the idea we have in our mind of how things 'should be' that stop us from embracing 'what is'.

We are a Universe of Mind, intricately linked through the energy that permeates all life.

My Wellbeing Universe is a resource to help young people navigate this fast-changing world and find an anchor within to their peace and stability. This journal is a non-linear, open-ended exploration of what it means to be well.

What we need to be well is ever-evolving, as we change individually and collectively. It's not a simple a-b-c linear, formulaic, one-size-fits-all approach, so it can't be taught like that.

The space I offer you is neutral, safe and exploratory. My hope with this resource is for the ideas to raise questions in your mind, inspire dialogue, strip away some of the limiting beliefs that box us into a fixed way of thinking and train the skills to be able to calm, centre and focus your mind.

I hope you enjoy the process of exploring these ideas as much as I enjoyed developing them.

Thank you for your support,

www.mywellbeingschool.com
@mywellbeingschool

foreword
BY DR NICKY HIRST

With the 2030 Sustainable Development agenda validating the importance of new ways of thinking and doing (UNESCO, 2015), this Well being journal for children provides opportunities for reflection and reflexivity which is much needed in the current global context with all the associated uncertainties regarding the future. The current Sustainable Development Goals (UNESCO, 2015-2030), focus on creating change that integrates the socio cultural, environmental and economic dimensions of sustainability recognised by the Brundtland World Commission in 1987. Critiques of this well -versed discourse '...meets the needs of the present without compromising the ability of future generations to meet their own needs' (Brundtland, 1987, 43), argue that this need focused perspective limits the idea of agency (Sudhir and Sen, 2000) and the concept of need remains 'overtly focused on development within existing capitalist systems' (Hunter et al, 2018, 16).

Heather eloquently describes My Wellbeing Universe as 'non- linear' and as a resource for 'open ended exploration of what it means to be well'. Heather was also keen to recognise existing journals for children and adults which have flooded social media platforms during the global Covid pandemic and subsequent collaborations with Liverpool John Moores University have also resulted in a student focused well being journal within the School of Education. In this online collaborative space, staff and interns worked with Heather to identify how meditation could be a tangible medium for well being and engagement with bespoke meditations embedded within the journal accessed via QR codes which students can access on their phones.

Heather was keen to acknowledge the plethora of useful sources which have inspired the development of My Wellbeing Universe and she gives due recognition to the UNCRC as a legally binding international agreement and with tacit nods to Deleuze and Guattari (1987, 1995), she carefully facilitates children's rights to own their journal.

My Wellbeing Universe opens up spaces and encourages 'nomadic' thinking (Deleuze and Guatarri, 1987, 1995), where the principles related to Education for sustainability and rhizomatic principles help to deterritorise current understandings and reterritorise new understandings (Tillmanns 2017, 32).

This cognisance of the UNCRC goes beyond an individual concept of 'rights' to promote what Julie Davis (2014) calls a revisioning of rights to an expanded rights framework where the journal aligns with pedagogies and principles of Education for Sustainability and reflects what Wals and Jickling (2008) characterise as the third approach to Education for sustainable development to enable thought and action. This moves beyond a simple notion of 'development' to explore self and moral questions, values and social justice.

I am delighted with the collaboration between My Wellbeing School and Liverpool John Moores University and we will continue to develop with some fruitful research as we pilot journaling for wellbeing with young children and students.

Dr Nicky Hirst

School of Education

Liverpool John Moores University UK

A look inside

Inside every cell and atom,
within each breath you take,
exists the wisdom of the
Universe.

Breathe in deeply,
it's time to explore.

Have you written your name on the front?

It's important because this is your journal.

A SAFE SPACE, FOR YOU TO EXPLORE THOUGHTS, FEELINGS AND IDEAS.

That means

There is no right or wrong answer here.

The key to using this journal is honesty with yourself.

SO DON'T WORRY ABOUT GETTING IT "RIGHT".

Draw, sketch, doodle, write and enjoy the journey into **My Wellbeing Universe**.

THE GOAL OF **My Wellbeing Universe** IS TO HELP YOU TRAIN THE SKILLS TO UNDERSTAND YOUR THOUGHTS, EMOTIONS AND DEVELOP THE COURAGE TO TRUST AND LISTEN TO YOURSELF.

Journaling is a powerful tool. It can help you make sense of the ideas in your mind and help you to get perspective on the feelings bubbling all over the place and see things a little clearer.

BE KIND TO YOURSELF

Try not to compare yourself with other people

You know yourself best

Be yourself

It takes courage to be yourself

EVERYONE IS UNIQUE

YOU ARE ALLOWED TO CHANGE YOUR MIND

BE HONEST WITH YOURSELF

It is OK not to know

Talking about your feelings is a sign of strength

EVERYONE HAS GOOD DAYS AND BAD DAYS

These are your journal pages.
They mark the beginning of a new chapter.
Here are a few tips on how to use them.

Remember this is your journal.
You don't have to share your work with anyone if you don't want to. Sometimes it's helpful to talk and share how you are feeling.

Thought bubble
What is going on inside your mind today? Write, draw or doodle.

date:
today in my world...

Today in my world...
Write or draw anything that is going on in your life that is important to you.

Empty face
You might like to draw how you feel on the face or write a few words, make a doodle or even a scribble if that is how you are feeling.

i am grateful for:

Why gratitude?
Gratitude is about appreciating the good things in our life. It is an attitude that can change how we feel; from focusing on the negative stuff and feeling miserable, to noticing even the smallest things in our lives to be grateful for.

At the end of each chapter you will find a guided meditation.
You can either listen to the meditations on
www.mywellbeingschool.com/universe
or have someone read them aloud to you.

Very often when we feel angry, upset or anxious it can feel like our thoughts and feelings are swirling around inside us at a million miles an hour.

MEDITATION TRAINS US TO DIRECT OUR THOUGHTS AND SETTLE OUR EMOTIONS. THIS IS A SKILL THAT WILL LAST YOU A LIFETIME IF YOU KEEP PRACTISING. JUST ONE MINUTE A DAY OF CONSCIOUS BREATHING IS ENOUGH TO TRAIN AND STRENGTHEN YOUR MIND.

5 Tips on how to meditate:

1
TRY TO MAKE SURE THE PLACE YOU CHOOSE TO MEDITATE IN IS SILENT. LET OTHERS KNOW THAT YOU ARE GOING TO MEDITATE SO THEY DON'T START TALKING TO YOU. IF YOU HEAR NOISE AROUND YOU, JUST LET IT GUIDE YOU DEEPER INTO YOUR MEDITATION.

3
KEEP YOUR BREATHING RELAXED. TRY TO BREATHE DEEPLY INTO YOUR BELLY WHILST KEEPING YOUR SHOULDERS AND CHEST SOFT. SEE IF YOU CAN TIME YOUR BREATHING TO FOUR BEATS OF YOUR HEART AS YOU BREATHE IN AND FOUR BEATS OF YOUR HEART AS YOU BREATHE OUT.

2
IF YOU FIND IT HARD TO CONCENTRATE AND YOU KEEP THINKING ABOUT EVERYTHING ELSE UNDER THE SUN WHEN YOU CLOSE YOUR EYES TO MEDITATE, THAT'S NORMAL. LET YOUR THOUGHTS PASS LIKE CLOUDS AND COME BACK TO YOUR MEDITATION.

4
SIT OR LIE DOWN COMFORTABLY. KEEP YOUR BACK STRAIGHT TO ALLOW YOUR BREATHING TO BE RELAXED AND YOUR CIRCULATION TO FLOW.

5
MINDFULNESS IS THE ART OF BRIDGING THE GAP BETWEEN MEDITATION AND EVERYDAY LIFE. BRING THAT PEACEFUL STATE YOU FEEL AFTER YOUR MEDITATION WITH YOU FOR AS LONG AS YOU CAN. PRACTICE BEING MINDFUL AS YOU EAT, WALK OR DO ANY NUMBER OF TASKS.

let's do a guided meditation
www.mywellbeingschool.com/universe1

I am grateful

Scan me

I am grateful

Close your eyes. Take some deep comfortable breaths.

Allow your thoughts to settle, your emotions to calm, and simply concentrate on your breathing. Feel the air as it flows in through your nose or your mouth and down into your chest, cleaning the air inside your body. Concentrate as you breathe out, feeling your chest soften as the unclean air leaves your body.

As you continue to concentrate on your breathing, allow yourself to tune in to the beats of your heart. Feel the rhythm of your heart as you concentrate on your breathing. Soft and effortless.

Allow any noise you hear around you to guide you deeper into your meditation, as you focus on each breath, and each beat of your heart.

Now bring to mind what you are grateful for today. Perhaps you are grateful for certain people in your life, or something about yourself; it could be an experience you've had or a particular object. Whatever it is that you are most grateful for, see it and experience it as clearly as you can.

See it in full high definition colour. What do you feel inside your body when you focus on gratitude? Observe it. Allow this feeling to flood through your entire body, filling every part of you, from the soles of your feet to the top of your head. Let the feeling of gratitude flow deep inside your body.

Now place your hands onto your chest and in your mind give thanks to your heart for beating every moment. Give thanks to your lungs for filling you with air.

As you breathe in deeply and feel the air entering your lungs once more, mentally say thank you to the air all around you that you share with everyone on the planet.

Breathe in deeply.

Feel this gratitude inside your bones, your blood, your cells.

When you are ready, you can open your eyes.

The key is you

"My friend,
- care for your psyche -
know thyself, for once we
know ourselves,
we may learn how to
care for ourselves."

Socrates

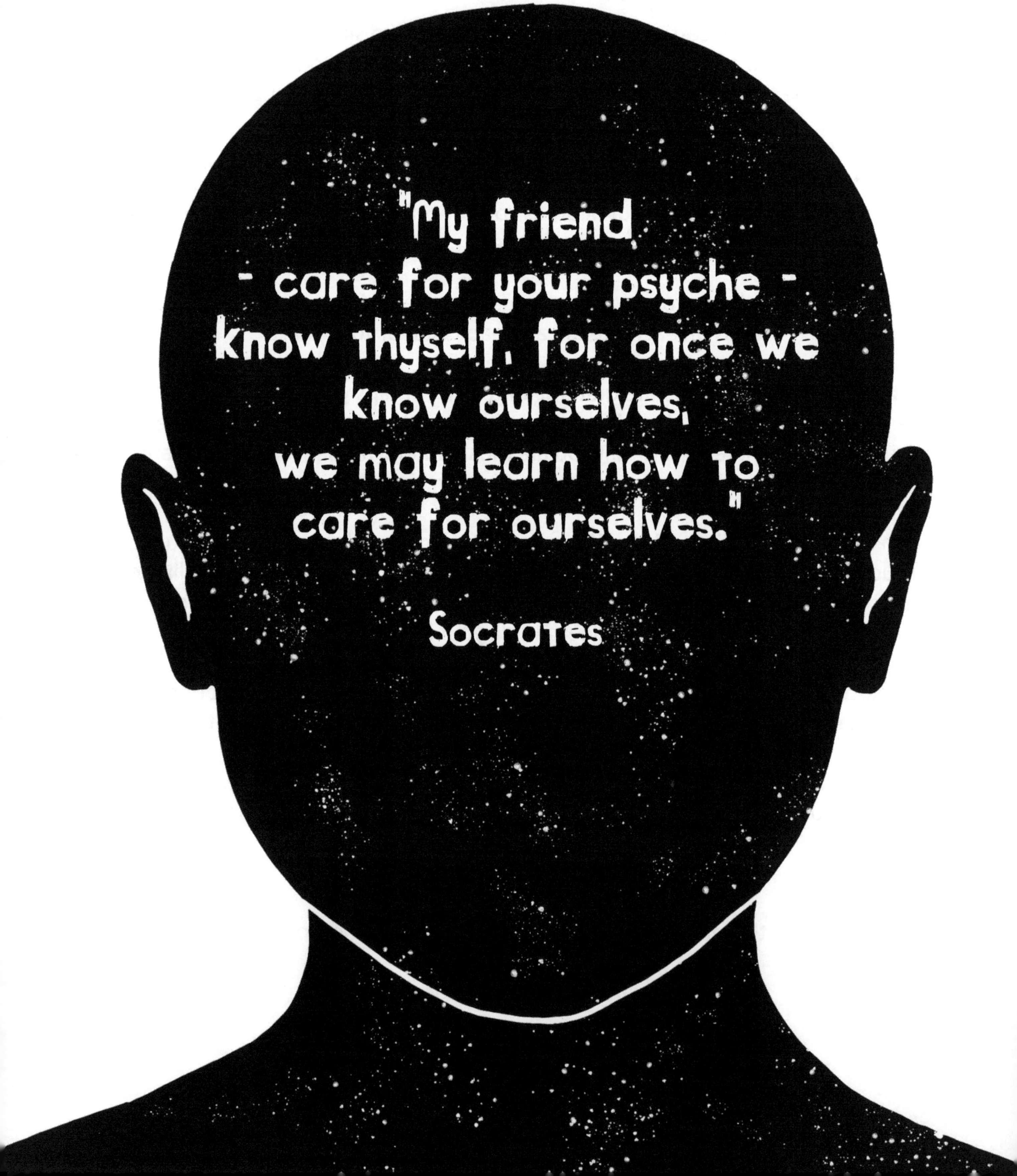

date:

today in my world...

i am grateful for:

Wellbeing is an action word

The **being** in wellbeing means it's something we have to live.

It also means that what makes you feel well changes as you grow and develop.

Wellbeing looks different for everyone.

It's a personal journey.

WHAT YOU NEED TO FEEL HAPPY, HEALTHY AND BALANCED MAY BE DIFFERENT TO OTHERS.

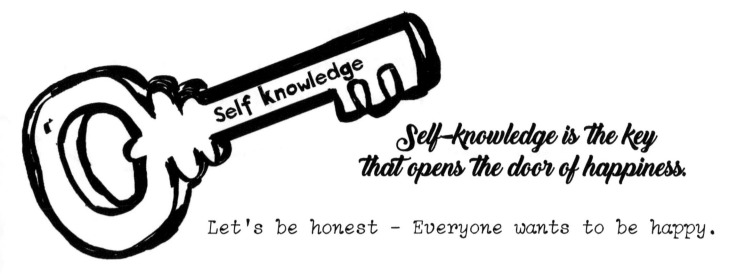

Self-knowledge is the key that opens the door of happiness.

Let's be honest - Everyone wants to be happy.

We all want to feel well.

Nobody wants to spend their life feeling rubbish, sad or angry. That's just no fun at all.

SADLY, SOME PEOPLE DO SPEND A LOT OF THEIR LIFE FEELING MISERABLE.

It has nothing to do with how much money or things they have because lasting happiness comes from within.

Understanding how to take care of your mental, emotional and physical wellbeing is the most important thing you will ever learn.

It's a journey within that only you can take.

Are you ready?

flash exercise: without thinking too much, write, sketch or talk out your answers to these questions. Time: one minute per question.

Who are you?

WHAT DO YOU LOVE ABOUT YOURSELF?

What gets you annoyed?

What is your biggest fear?

HOW DO YOU FEEL INSIDE MOST OF THE TIME?

What makes
you feel well?

What makes you nervous?

IF YOU COULD ACHIEVE ANYTHING
IN THE WORLD WHAT
WOULD IT BE?

Who are the important
people in your life?

What is the best feeling?

let's do a guided meditation

www.mywellbeingschool.com/universe2

I am well

Scan me

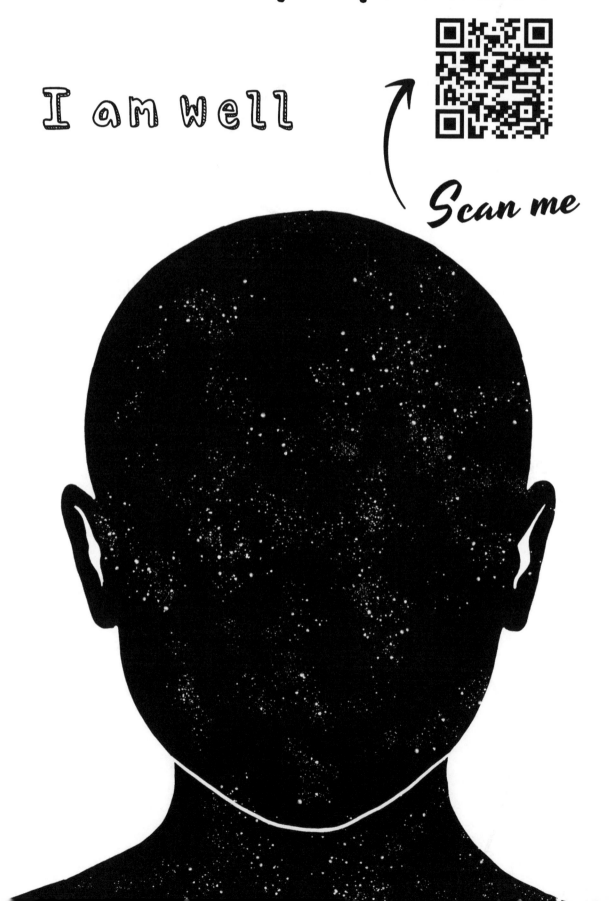

I am well

Close your eyes and take some deep, comfortable breaths.

Allow your mind to calm, your feelings to settle and enter the space inside of you.

Feel the beats of your material heart, as you continue to breathe deeply and comfortably.

Allow any noises around you to guide you deeper into your meditation as you feel your physical body relaxing and the space inside your mind clearing.

Now bring to mind what makes you feel well. Scan through in your mind what you wrote in your journal, the people, places, activities, food or things that help you feel well.

As you continue to breathe, this feeling of wellness spreads through your entire body like a river of warmth rushing through you.

Concentrate on this feeling.

Slowly you notice that your body begins radiating a sky-blue light, as bright as the sky on a perfect summer's day.

This light of wellness flows through your body, like a powerful river, charging up your body, your heart and your mind with health and energy.

Breathe in this feeling.

Now when you are ready, open your eyes.

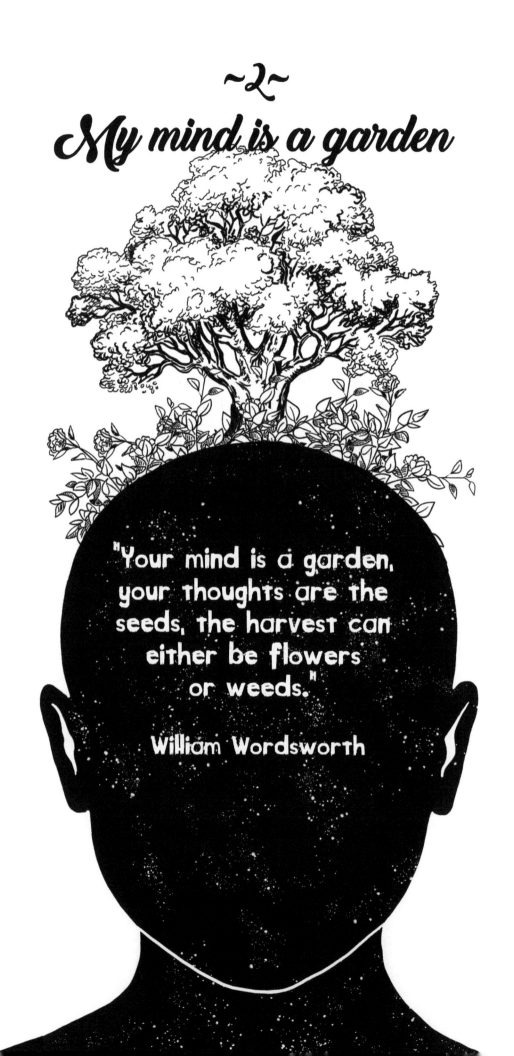

~2~

My mind is a garden

"Your mind is a garden,
your thoughts are the
seeds, the harvest can
either be flowers
or weeds."

William Wordsworth

Every thought we have is a seed.
What do seeds need to grow?

FLOWERS ARE THE POSITIVE THOUGHTS THAT HELP US BLOSSOM INTO THE BEST VERSIONS OF OURSELVES.

A WEED IS A NEGATIVE THOUGHT THAT TAKES OVER YOUR GARDEN.

Sunlight is the attention we put on these thoughts.

Water is our actions to help nurture them.

Conditions are how open your mind is to allowing these thoughts to take root and the support you have from people around you.

28

It's very hard for anything but weeds to grow through the concrete of a **fixed-mindset.**

Flowers blossom in a **growth-mindset.** A Mind filled with postivive thoughts nurtures a positive life.

Thoughts are powerful.
We create the conditions in our mind by the way we think and talk to ourselves.

Be aware of the seeds planted in our minds by others. Our family, friends, teachers and culture all contribute to what we think about ourselves and the world around us.

Now is the moment you choose what type of garden you want to grow in your mind.

What weeds do you want to uproot?
What seeds do you want to plant?

IT'S YOUR MIND AND YOUR GARDEN.

You are the one that has to listen to your thoughts everyday. You are the one that lives in your mind, nobody else.

SO MAKE IT AN AMAZING PLACE TO BE!

Words have power - so let's use them.

Sometimes it can be hard to 'change' our mindset because we get used to thinking in a certain way. Just like anything new it takes practice.

Meditation is a powerful tool for training your mind and focusing your thoughts.

ANOTHER WAY TO TRAIN OUR THOUGHTS IS USING AN AUTO-SUGGESTION.

A SHORT SENTENCE ABOUT THE WAY YOU WANT TO FEEL, THINK AND LIVE.

Using an auto-suggestion or 'mantra' is a great way to redirect your thoughts and focus the sunlight of your mind onto the flowers you want to grow.

Write or draw the thoughts you want to nurture in the garden of your mind.

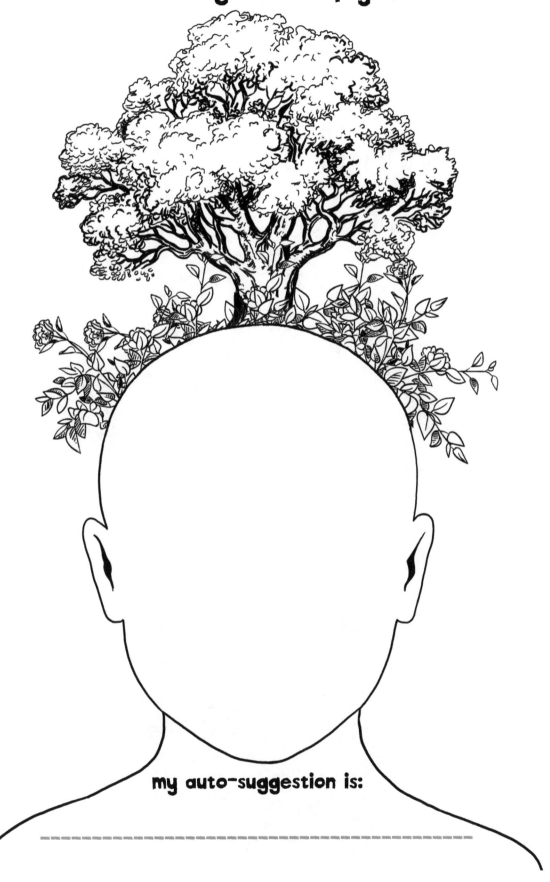

my auto-suggestion is:

_____

_____

_____

let's do a guided meditation

www.mywellbeingschool.com/universe3

My mind is
a garden

Scan me

My mind is a garden

Close your eyes and relax. Take some deep comfortable breaths.

With every breath you take, you feel your mind, emotions and body calming, relaxing into the present moment as you attune and feel the beats of your heart.

Now visualise and see yourself, standing in a garden. Your body is dressed in bright white light. Take a moment as you observe this garden of your mind, on a warm spring morning. Flowers in bloom all around you, rich sweet smells hit that back of your nostrils and you breathe it in. You feel the cool air, notice it flowing through the leaves softly in the trees. This is the garden in your mind. And every thought you've ever had was a seed, planted here, watered and nourished by the attention you have given it.

Take yourself for a walk around the garden. Observe the flowers and the trees. A rose bush calls your attention. As you walk towards it, you lean in and smell its deep sweet scent. You feel it connecting to your heart, to the love you have for yourself, for those in your life that are special to you.

Sometimes relationships aren't easy, but always we focus on coming back to the love inside ourselves and that love will spread. Give thanks to this rose bush and for the people in your life that help nurture this garden.

Now further to the back is a large oak tree, with a strong firm trunk. As you walk towards it and place your hands on its rough bark, you feel the stable grounding energy of this oak tree. Who you are was planted at birth, grown through every experience, every storm, resilient with roots growing deep into the earth and branches reaching up to the sky. Give thanks to this tree as you attune to its stability and strength.

As you wander deeper into your garden, the weeds start to grow a little wild. Shadows sprawling out, overtaking parts of your garden. Walk towards these weeds, as you do you carry an inner light, and they recoil slightly away from the brightness of the light shining inside you. These weeds that have been allowed to grow wild are the thoughts that hold you back, the negative thoughts that do not serve you. If we give our attention and energy to them, they will overtake the garden of our mind.

Kneel down and place your hand firmly at the base of one of these weeds. As you pull it out you place your other hand on the hole where you pulled it, and charge the earth with the white light from within your body, filling the hole with love. Do this to every weed that is growing, pull them out one by one and place them in a pile in the centre of your garden.

These weeds do not serve you. As you notice the pile of weeds in the centre of your garden and you stand beside them, you feel the warmth of the sun shining down onto your body, you notice a golden ray of light shining from the sun, connecting to this pile of weeds and lighting them up in golden flames. Stand and observe this golden bonfire, notice any smoke that is leaving. As the light dies down and the ashes are all that remains, you look in the palms of your hands and see a seed. A new intention, a new thought. What is this seed for you? Attune with it and listen. Kneel and dig a hole in the earth, as you plant this seed, you cover it with the rich ash of the weeds, charge it up with your energy and love. This is your mind and your garden and you choose what grows here. You can come back anytime and watch this seed as it grows, spend time walking around and observing.
Breathe in deeply and slowly feel yourself coming back to your material body
and whenever you are ready, open your eyes.

~3~
My emotions are the weather

feelings come and go,
like clouds on a stormy day.
You are not the clouds,
you are the sky

date:

today in my world...

i am grateful for:

Just like the weather changes, so do our emotions. Learning to navigate through stormy weather means that you will find your way back to yourself when your emotional weather calms down.

SOME EMOTIONS FILL US WITH AN ENERGY THAT FEELS GREAT, LIKE A WARM SUMMER'S AFTERNOON.

SOME EMOTIONS MAKE IT HARD TO SEE CLEARLY, LIKE A FOG THAT MAKES EVERYTHING MURKY

SOME EMOTIONS CAN FEEL LIKE YOU ARE BEING JUMBLED AND TUMBLED INSIDE A TORNADO.

It's OK if you're not OK. As long as you don't stay that way!

SOME EMOTIONS FEEL AS THOUGH YOUR ENTIRE BODY IS ON FIRE FROM INSIDE

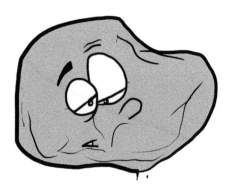

SOME EMOTIONS FEEL LIKE HEAVY ROCKS WEIGHING YOU DOWN

Even though emotions happen inside of us, the feelings they give us are very real.

EMOTIONS ARE IMPORTANT, THEY HELP US SURVIVE. OUR BRAIN RELEASES DIFFERENT CHEMICALS IN OUR BODY ACCORDING TO THE EMOTIONS WE FEEL.

If we feel afraid our brain releases adrenaline and cortisol which makes our heart pump faster giving us extra energy to outrun or fight off danger.

i don't like this...run!

Love makes us feel connected to people, it helps us take care of others selflessly. When you give someone a hug you are filling your body with feel-good hormones. The chemicals of love are oxytocin, dopamine, and serotonin.

this feels much better!

Emotions are our feelings. How WE feel about things.

Does everyone feel the same about different things?

WHAT MAKES ONE PERSON SCARED MIGHT MAKE SOMEONE ELSE FEEL EXCITED.

SO HOW WE FEEL AND REACT TO OUTSIDE SITUATIONS IS A VERY PERSONAL THING.

Some people feel lots of emotional ups and downs.

EMOTIONS GIVE US DIFFERENT ENERGY.

SOME PEOPLE SEEM TO BE ALWAYS HAPPY.

Emotions like love, joy, excitement, open your mind and fill you with more energy and creative thinking.

It's just a part of being human.

OTHER PEOPLE SEEM LIKE THEY ARE ALWAYS GRUMPY.

Emotions like anger, sadness, fear, leave you less motivated, you have less creativity and focus.

AT THE END OF THE DAY, YOU HAVE TO DECIDE WHAT WORKS BEST FOR YOU.

Do you want to feel happy or grumpy?

IT'S ALL ABOUT HOW WE REACT INSIDE TO THE WORLD OUTSIDE OF US.

You don't have to be any which way - you can just be you.

YOU ARE THE ONE THAT LIVES INSIDE YOUR BODY. YOU ARE THE ONE THAT GETS TO FEEL THE BUZZ OF EXCITEMENT OR THE BURN OF ANGER.

Having the words to describe how we feel.

Feelings can be hard to understand. Sometimes we don't even know why or what we are feeling, we just know that we don't feel good. Talking about how you feel, even if you don't have the perfect words to describe them, helps decode your feelings.

Opening up to others helps them understand us more, and just by talking things through we begin to shine a light on the situation and it will help you start feeling better.

IN YOUR OWN WORDS TALK TO SOMEONE ABOUT HOW THESE EMOTIONS MAKE YOU FEEL AND THEN DRAW A LINE ACROSS THE PAGE FROM EACH WORD TO ILLUSTRATE HOW EACH EMOTION LOOKS TO YOU. REMEMBER, THERE IS NO RIGHT OR WRONG.

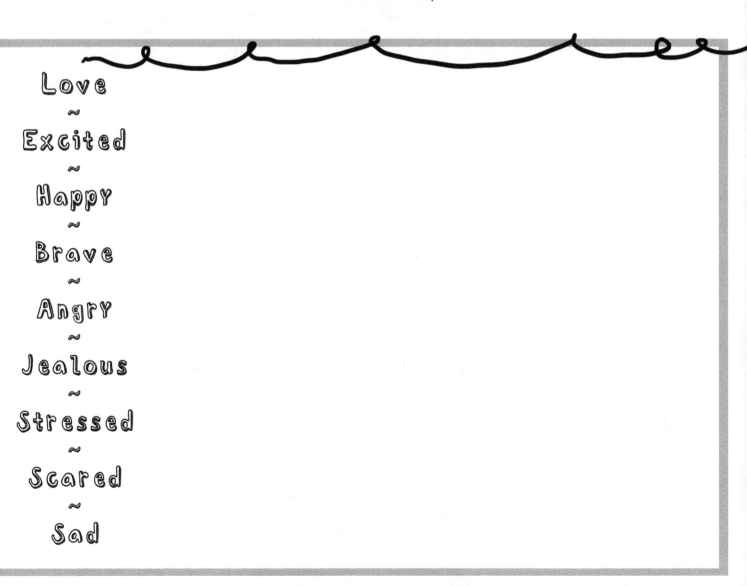

Love
~
Excited
~
Happy
~
Brave
~
Angry
~
Jealous
~
Stressed
~
Scared
~
Sad

let's do a guided meditation

www.mywellbeingschool.com/universe4

My emotional weather

Scan me

My emotional Weather

Close your eyes and take some deep comfortable breaths.

Allow your mind to calm, your emotions to balance as you connect to the beats of your heart and the rhythm of your breath.

Visualise and see yourself, sitting on a cliff, looking out onto the horizon. The sun is setting, the clouds in the sky are tinged with pinks and orange. The air is still, cool and crisp as you breathe in. Today has been a turbulent day.

Lie on your back now and look up at the sky, observe the clouds passing, the sun setting. The emotions you feel are much like the weather. The pressure builds, we change and they are a part of being human, of expressing yourself in this world.

It's OK to feel the storms and enjoy the sunsets. As you learn to find a stillness inside yourself to observe your emotions like the weather and to know that if clouds are covering you today, the sun still shines behind them.

The clouds will pass and the rain will come and it will wash you clean. And as you feel this peaceful sunset, filling you up with a deep appreciation and love for the life you have, you breathe it in and feel it entering into every cell and atom of your being.

You place your hand on your heart and feel a rainbow of light shining from your heart connecting to the sun. A ray of yourself shining in this light; always present, always found with every breath you take and beat of your heart.

Breathe in deeply and slowly feel yourself coming back to the feeling of your material body. Feel the rainbow in your heart lighting you up from within and carry this feeling with you for the rest of the week.

~4~

A new pair of glasses

Things change when you change the way you look at them.

So much of our happiness depends on how we choose to view the world.

YOU DECIDE!

Imagine you are looking through a pair of glasses

The lenses make everything look blurry, they are scratched, dark and it's hard to see through them. When you put the glasses on they make you feel frustrated and annoyed.
These are your "life is rubbish glasses".

Now imagine another pair of glasses.

These lenses are tinted a light blue, whenever you put those glasses on, suddenly everything feels calm, even when people are arguing in front of you, with the cool blue glasses you manage to keep your calm, cool feelings.

How about a pair of life is awesome glasses.
These glasses are rosy tinted and make everything amazing. Nothing can get you down when you wear these glasses and you can achieve anything you want when you put your mind to it.

These golden glasses help you solve any problem. Whenever you put them on you feel your mind opening and your creative genius flowing through you.

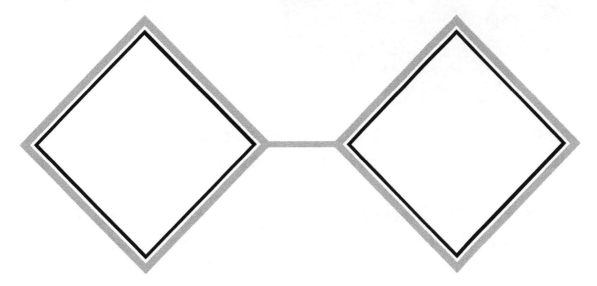

Imagine if it were that simple.

OH WAIT! HANG ON... IT REALLY IS.

Our eyes are our lenses and the way we see the world comes from what we look for. Our thoughts and feelings about each situation colour the way we experience each moment.

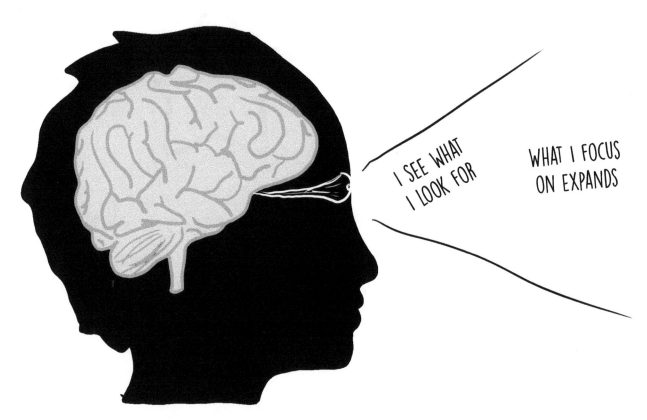

Some people see the danger in everything because they focus on fear. The world becomes a scary place to live in.

Others look for the kindness in others, because they focus on love, those are the people that bring out the good in others.

SO EVERYDAY, WHEN YOU WAKE UP IN THE MORNING, CHOOSE THE GLASSES YOU WANT TO PUT ON.

This is called setting an intention. Choosing the lens that you want to see the world through.

Draw your glasses and set your intention.
HOW DO YOU WANT TO SEE THE WORLD?

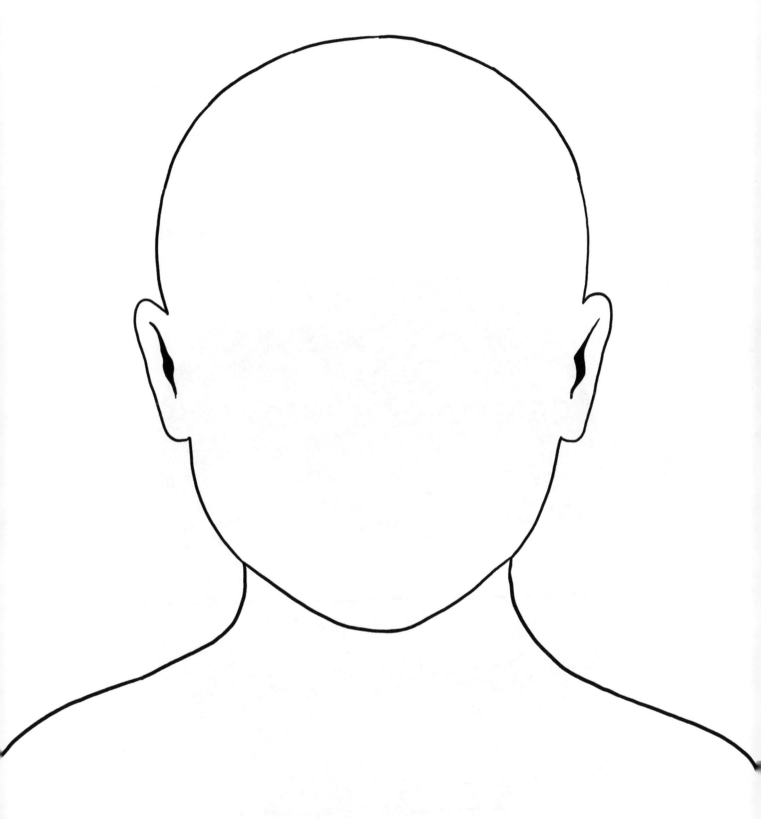

let's do a guided meditation

www.mywellbeingschool.com/universe5

A new pair of glasses

Scan me

48

A new pair of glasses

Close your eyes and take some deep comfortable breaths.

With every breath you take, you feel your mind and emotions calming down, as you connect to the beats of your heart and the rhythm of your breath.

Now imagine you are lying in your bed, first thing in the morning. You reach to put your glasses on, the glasses you wear today are blurry, scratched and it's hard to see. Imagine yourself going through your morning, having breakfast, speaking with people in your home, heading to school; all the while feeling frustrated and annoyed that these glasses don't let you see clearly.

You get to halfway through the day, and decide enough is enough. You don't want to wear these scratched, blurry glasses. You don't want to feel annoyed or frustrated or angry. So you take the glasses off and throw them away.

In your hands appear another pair of glasses. Take a moment to observe and see this new pair of glasses you hold in your hands.

How do they feel? What do they look like? What colour are the lenses?

You decide to put them on, and as you slowly slide these glasses on and look through the lenses, you feel suddenly lit up from inside.

Everything feels so much brighter and clearer. And as you go through the rest of your day, you feel a smile spread from inside your heart. An openness and creativity in your mind that you have never felt before. Life feels amazing through these glasses.

As you slowly feel yourself returning to the space and awareness of your physical body, in a moment when you open your eyes, imagine you are still wearing these glasses and allow the world to be lit up. Breathe deeply and whenever you are ready, open your eyes.

5

My inner senses

Trust yourself,
you are much more
powerful than you think.

Our five senses help us survive and connect us to the world around us.

These five senses also can turn inwardly, they connect us to the world inside of us.

Touch – WE FEEL THE WORLD THROUGH OUR SENSE OF TOUCH.

WE ALSO FEEL OUR EMOTIONS THROUGH OUR INNER TOUCH.

HOW MUCH WE UNDERSTAND THESE FEELINGS IS HOW IN TOUCH WE ARE WITH OURSELVES.

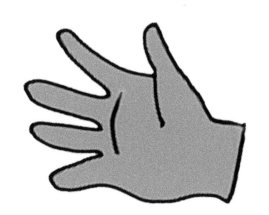

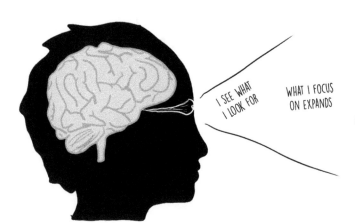

I SEE WHAT I LOOK FOR

WHAT I FOCUS ON EXPANDS

Sight – OUR EYES HELP US SEE. WE CAN ALSO SEE WHEN WE CLOSE OUR EYES. WE CAN SEE THESE IMAGES THAT FORM IN OUR MIND WITH OUR INNER EYE.

It's interesting that our brain can't tell the difference between what we remember we have seen and what we imagine. The same part of your brain activates when you remember and when you imagine. Your inner sight is linked to the idea we explored in the last chapter, what we focus on expands. what we look for we find.

Sound — THE WORLD SPEAKS TO US, BUT WE ALSO SPEAK TO OURSELVES. LEARNING TO LISTEN AND TRUST YOURSELF IS A SUPERPOWER, IT GIVES YOU THE STRENGTH TO BE YOURSELF. YOU CARE LESS ABOUT WHAT OTHERS THINK ABOUT YOU BECAUSE YOU HAVE TURNED UP THE VOLUME ON YOUR VOICE.

WE HAVE TO BE STILL TO LISTEN, AND THAT'S WHERE MEDITATION COMES IN VERY HANDY. WE LET THE NOISE SETTLE, ALL THE VOICES AND OPINIONS OF OTHERS SETTLE TO THE BOTTOM AND WE CAN HEAR OUR VOICE SHINING THROUGH.

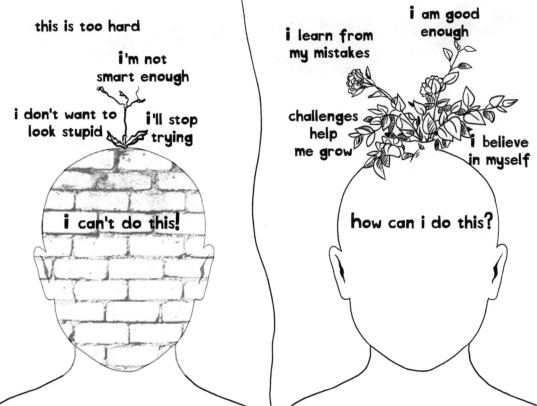

The words WE SAY TO OURSELVES HAVE POWER. JUST LIKE THE DIFFERENCE BETWEEN A GROWTH MINDSET AND A FIXED MINDSET. WE BELIEVE WHAT WE TELL OURSELVES. IF YOU SAY YOU CAN'T FOR LONG ENOUGH, YOU NEVER WILL. REMEMBER EVERY THOUGHT WE HAVE IS A SEED AND WE NOURISH THOSE SEEDS WITH OUR ATTENTION. CHECK THE CONVERSATION GOING ON IN YOUR HEAD. ARE YOU NURTURING WEEDS OR FLOWERS?

Our breath CONNECTS THE WORLD OUTSIDE US TO THE WORLD INSIDE US.

WHEN WE FOCUS ON OUR BREATH, THROUGH MINDFULNESS OR MEDITATION WE ALLOW OUR THOUGHTS, FEELINGS AND PHYSICAL BODY TO CALM DOWN AND RELAX, THIS BRINGS US INTO THE PRESENT MOMENT, AND THAT MOMENT IS WHERE WE FIND ALL THE GOOD THINGS.

present moment

past

Worrying about something I did

Angry or upset about what happened

Sad because I'm thinking of things I no longer have

doing something you love

enjoying being with my friends or family

learning something new

facing challenges with courage

future

Anxious about what might happen

Insecure about what others might think about me

Stressed about something that might happen

grateful for life

What things, activities, thoughts, people or places pull you into the present moment?

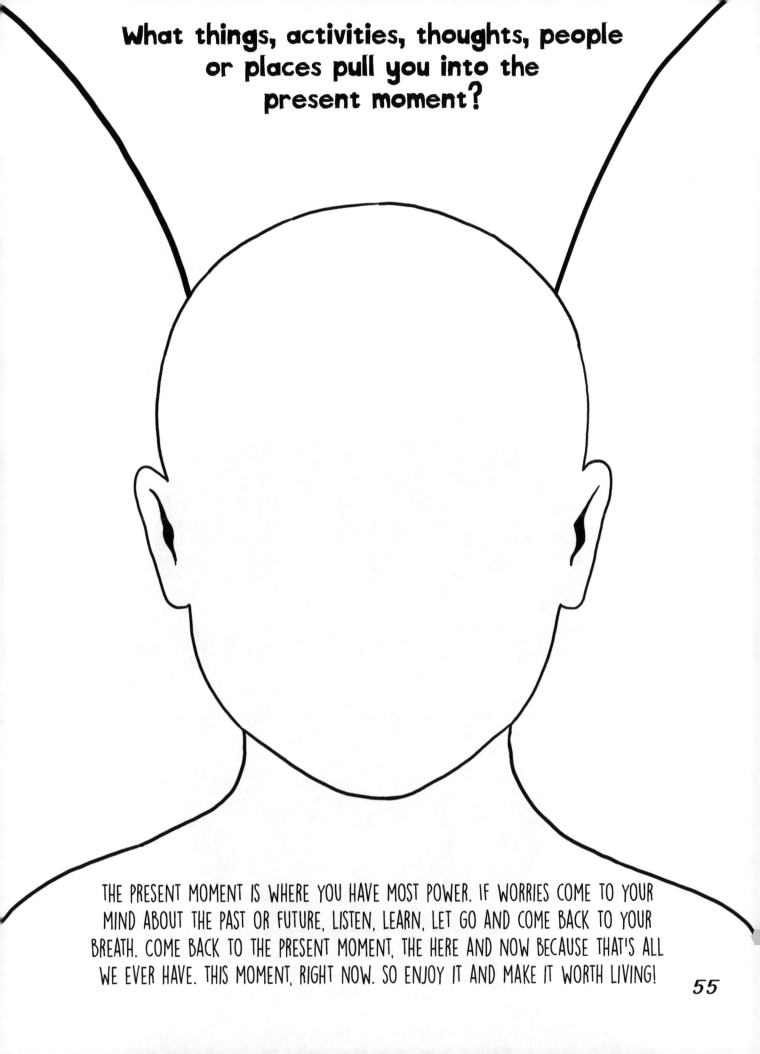

THE PRESENT MOMENT IS WHERE YOU HAVE MOST POWER. IF WORRIES COME TO YOUR MIND ABOUT THE PAST OR FUTURE, LISTEN, LEARN, LET GO AND COME BACK TO YOUR BREATH. COME BACK TO THE PRESENT MOMENT, THE HERE AND NOW BECAUSE THAT'S ALL WE EVER HAVE. THIS MOMENT, RIGHT NOW. SO ENJOY IT AND MAKE IT WORTH LIVING!

let's do a guided meditation

www.mywellbeingschool.com/universe6

The Present Moment

Scan me

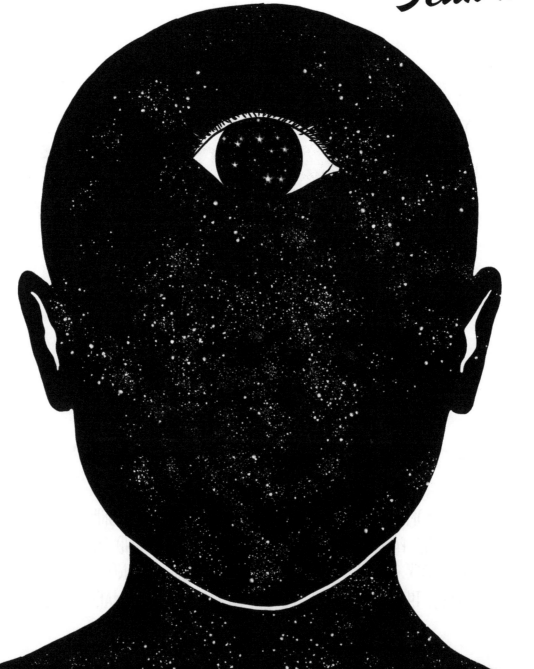

The present moment

Close your eyes and take some deep comfortable breaths.

Allow your mind to calm, your emotions to balance and feel the beats of your heart and the rhythm of your breath, guiding you deeper into an awareness of yourself. Place your awareness now into the soles of both your feet. Feel the soles of your feet and see a bright white light shining. Both your feet are now radiating a bright white light, you can see it with your inner eye.

Feel this light with your inner touch and move this feeling up through your calves and into your knees.

Allow this light and energy to spread all the way up into your head, flow down into your arms and fingertips until your entire body is shining in the bright white light.

Breathe consciously, and feel the present moment, feel this present moment in every cell and atom relaxing your body and your mind, as the light inside you expands beyond your body. Feel it spreading through the room, through your community, flowing through your entire body till the planet is bathed in this bright white light.

This present moment you feel, links you to every human being on the planet. Breathing the same air, the beats of their heart sustaining their life. And you feel a ray of the sun shining, lighting you up in golden radiation. And this golden light flows inside your body, and it opens you up to your own voice, to your inner guidance, and gives you the strength to trust and listen to yourself.

Breathe in deeply, and feel the light and energy and strength that comes as you attune to this present moment, as you turn your eyes inwardly.

You are peaceful, life-loving and content. Breathe in deeply, and bring this present moment with you, for the rest of your day.

6

The secret of my centre

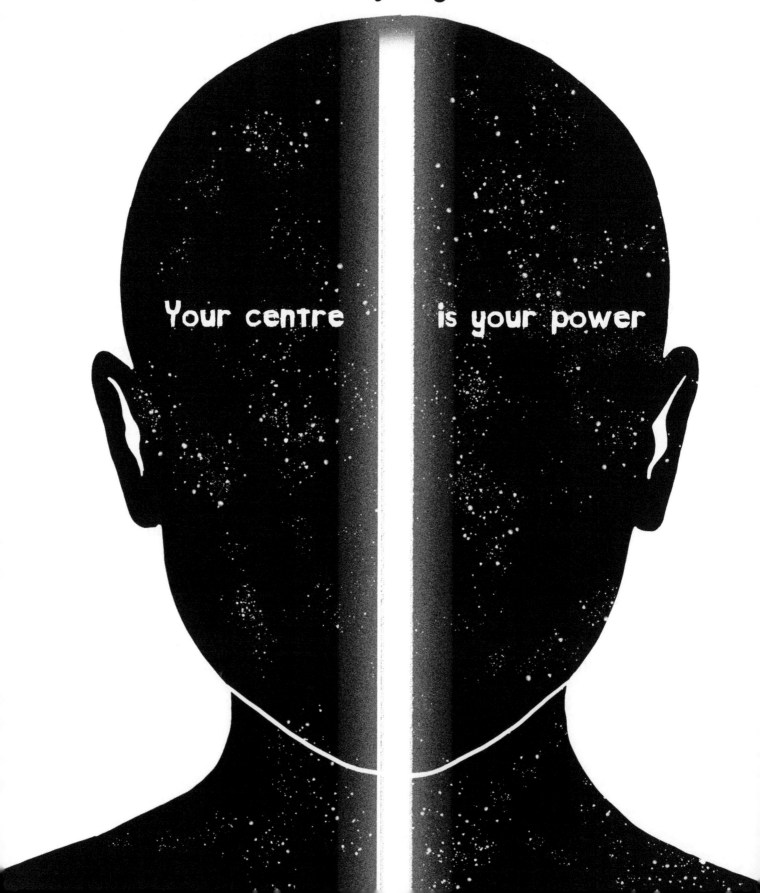

Your centre   is your power

finding Your Centre

1. MARK A POINT ON THIS DIAGRAM IN YELLOW TO SHOW WHERE **you think** IS THE CENTRE OF YOUR THOUGHTS.

2. NOW IN PINK MARK WHERE **you think** IS THE CENTRE OF YOUR FEELINGS.

3. NOW IN BLUE SHOW WHERE **you think** THE CENTRE OF YOUR BODY IS.

4. NOW DRAW A LINE CONNECTING THESE THREE CENTRES

Now turn the page and let's explore the **power of your centre.**

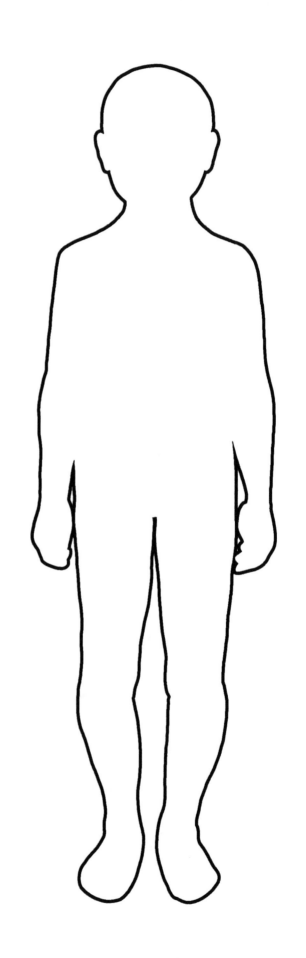

60

Did your diagram look something like this?

THE CENTRE OF OUR THOUGHTS IS OUR BRAIN *that was probably too easy*

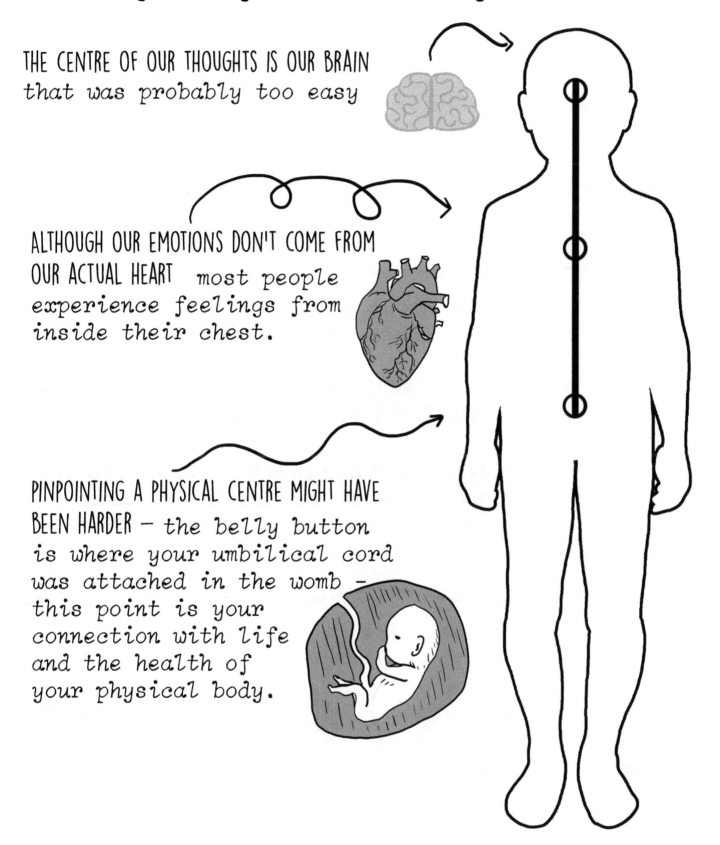

ALTHOUGH OUR EMOTIONS DON'T COME FROM OUR ACTUAL HEART *most people experience feelings from inside their chest.*

PINPOINTING A PHYSICAL CENTRE MIGHT HAVE BEEN HARDER – *the belly button is where your umbilical cord was attached in the womb – this point is your connection with life and the health of your physical body.*

What is the line running through each centre of your body?

When all these three centres are aligned you are at your most powerful. **When your head, heart and body are in the same place, you are in the present moment.**

PAUSE — NOW THINK ABOUT WHAT MAKES YOU HAPPIEST,

WHEN YOU ARE DOING THAT THING, OR WITH THAT PERSON, ARE YOU THINKING ABOUT ANYTHING ELSE?

DO YOU WANT TO BE ANYWHERE ELSE? HOW DO YOU FEEL?

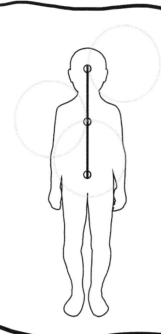

How about when you are doing something you don't want to do?

ARE YOU THINKING ABOUT HOW MUCH YOU DON'T WANT TO BE DOING IT? MAYBE THINKING ABOUT WHAT YOU WOULD RATHER BE DOING?

Your Mind and heart are in a different place to your body and this makes us unbalanced and weaker.

An experiment on structure:

GET AN EGG AND PRESS FIRMLY ON THE TOP AND BOTTOM.

TRY PRESSING EVEN HARDER... DOES THE EGG BREAK?

NOW CHANGE THE WAY YOU HOLD THE EGG. PRESS DOWN ON THE MIDDLE OF THE EGG.

WHAT HAPPENED? WHAT DOES THIS SHOW YO[U] ABOUT ALIGNMENT?

Remember the line you drew that connected your three centres? Yes that's your Spine.

YOUR SPINE IS **flexible**, NOT RIGID.

THE BONES IN YOUR SPINE ARE CALLED VERTEBRAE. BETWEEN EACH VERTEBRA IS A DISC FILLED WITH 80% WATER.

THESE HELP YOU TO BEND AND TWIST ALMOST ANY WAY YOU LIKE!

WITHOUT OUR SPINE WE WOULDN'T BE ABLE TO STAND UP. OUR SPINE GIVES US **support**.

A healthy spine is:

Flexible

Connective

strong

balanced

supportive

aligned

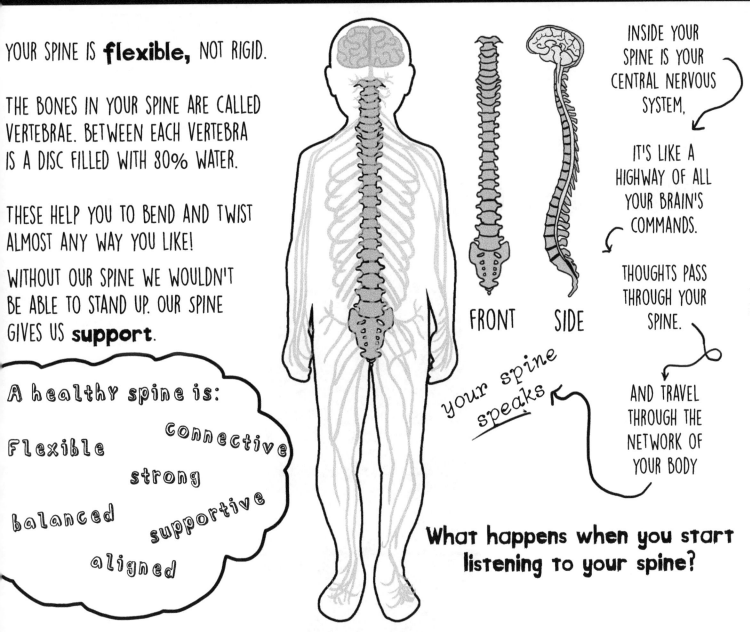

FRONT   SIDE

your spine speaks

INSIDE YOUR SPINE IS YOUR CENTRAL NERVOUS SYSTEM,

IT'S LIKE A HIGHWAY OF ALL YOUR BRAIN'S COMMANDS.

THOUGHTS PASS THROUGH YOUR SPINE.

AND TRAVEL THROUGH THE NETWORK OF YOUR BODY

What happens when you start listening to your spine?

When you connect to your centre and listen to your spine you enter into the present moment, aligning your head, heart and body.

SOME EXERCISES THAT IMPROVE YOUR SPINAL CONNECTION: SWIMMING

DANCE   YOGA   HORSE RIDING   KUNG FU   PILATES

Tip: Just thinking about your spine improves your connection

let's do a guided meditation

www.mywellbeingschool.com/universe7

Centred
Balanced
Powerful

Scan me

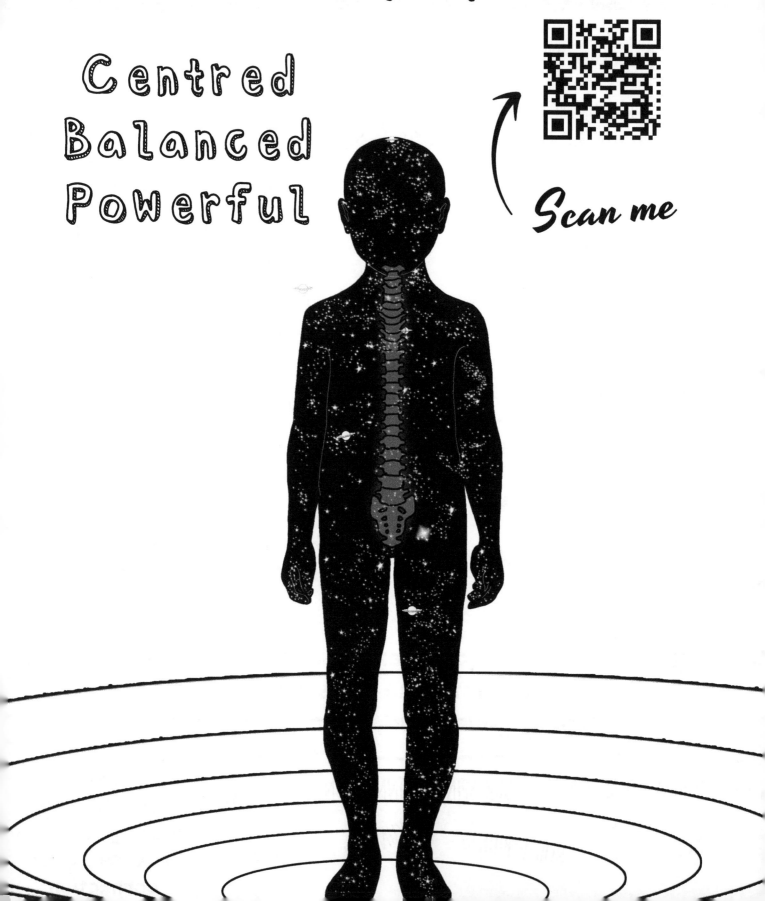

Centred, Balanced, Powerful

Close your eyes and take some deep comfortable breaths.

With every breath you take, feel your mind calming, your emotions settling as you enter deeper into an awareness of your Self.

Breathe deeply.

And bring your awareness to the crown of your head. Focus all your attention only on the top of your head. Now imagine you are standing in the shower and feel warm water flowing down your back, relaxing all your muscles completely.

And you feel this water travelling down your spine.

Now feel your spine from the base all the way to the top.

Imagine a hosepipe of water plugged into the base of your spine and through it flows a channel of clear white sparkling water through your entire spine, flowing out from the crown of your head.

You are like a human fountain. Feel the water flowing through your spine, pouring out from the crown of your head and then recycling back to your feet and travelling up again.

Feel yourself taller, totally relaxed. Connected to your inner power and strength.

You are peaceful, you are powerful, you are present.

Now bring this feeling with you for the rest of the week.

~7~
Freedom Thinking

"Why fit in when you
are born to stand out?"

Dr Seuss

The world is a diverse place.

Diverse means:
THERE'S LOTS OF DIFFERENT TYPES OF THINGS.

Think about all the different plants and animals there are in the wolrd.

Now imagine how boring life would be if there was only one type of tree, one type of food, one type of animal.

Variety is the spice of life.

BUT IT'S NOT JUST PLANTS AND ANIMALS THAT COME IN ALL SHAPES AND SIZES — SO DO WE.

It's not just the way we look that is different

WHAT WE ENJOY

the way we think

the way we see the world

the experiences we've had

Diversity is something to celebrate!

Diverse families

Every family looks different.

Some families have:

WHAT MIGHT BE ACCEPTABLE IN ONE FAMILY, COULD GET YOU INTO SERIOUS TROUBLE IN ANOTHER.

one parent

someone with a disability

lots of children

people with different religious beliefs

lots of laughter

two Mums

SOMEONE WHO HAS DIED

lots of people under one roof

SOMEONE WHO IS ILL

people that speak different languages

a small flat

loads of money

people that do not get on

PROBLEMS WITH MONEY

lots of pets

divorced parents

adopted children

two Dads

UNFORTUNATELY, SOME PEOPLE BELIEVE THAT IF YOU THINK DIFFERENTLY, ACT DIFFERENTLY OR LOOK DIFFERENT TO WHAT THEY ARE USED TO – IT'S WRONG.

This is called prejudice

it's a lot like having a fixed mindset

because you can't see another person's point of view.

Just because it's different doesn't mean it's wrong.

WHAT'S 'WRONG' IS TRYING TO FORCE OTHER PEOPLE TO THINK THE SAME WAY AS YOU, OR BULLYING THEM IF THEY ARE DIFFERENT.

If you think you know, very often you can't see.

THERE ARE PEOPLE WHO DON'T BELIEVE IN LIMITATIONS, WHO PAVE THE WAY FOR HUMAN PROGRESS. IT TAKES A SPECIAL MIND TO BELIEVE IN SOMETHING THAT HAS NEVER BEEN DONE BEFORE. TO BE A FORCE FOR GOOD ON THE PLANET, THEY ARE THE

Freedom Thinkers

Most people see only what they are told to see.

the world is flat

freedom thinkers – ask questions and make their own path

hmmm... I'm not so sure

Believe in the power of the mind

Able to step outside the box of limitation

DON'T ACCEPT OTHER PEOPLE'S OPINION AS FACT

Don't believe in failure

never give up

challenge the 'status-quo'

What would you do if you knew you couldn't fail?

Freedom begins with you

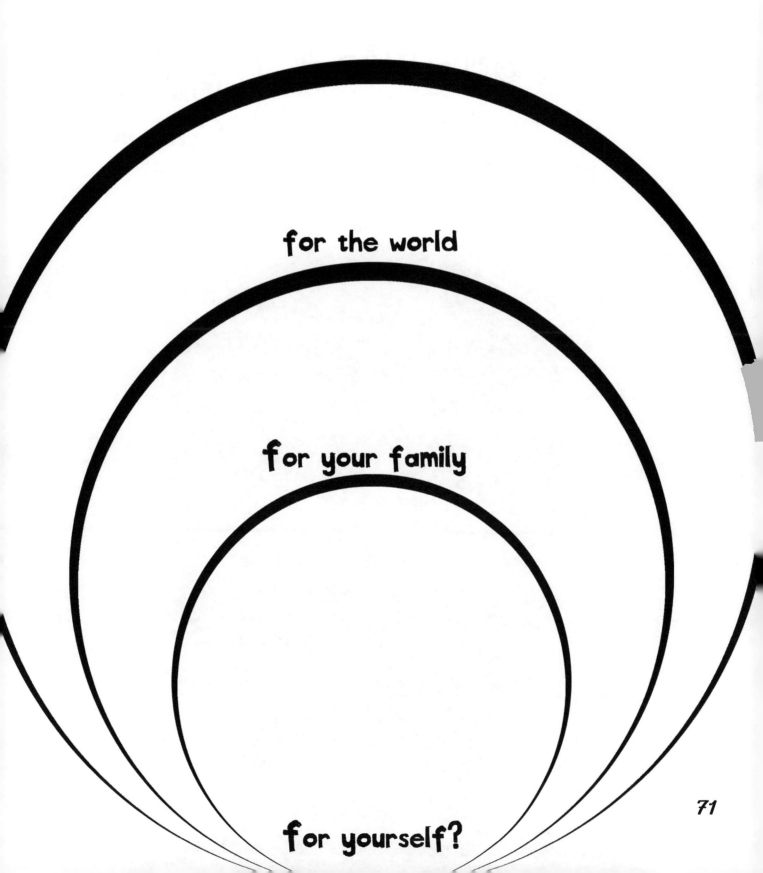

for the world

for your family

for yourself?

71

let's do a guided meditation

www.mywellbeingschool.com/universe8

Free Your Mind

Scan me

72

Free Your Mind

Close your eyes and take some deep conscious breaths

Allow your mind to calm with every breath you take.

As you breathe in, feel the air as it enters your lungs and flows through your body, washing it clean.

As you breathe out, you release the unclean air. Now visualise from the centre of your head a tiny ball of bright white light. Just the size of a spark.

With every breath you take this tiny spark of light grows brighter and clearer until your entire head is covered in a radiant golden light.

As you continue to softly concentrate on this light, you feel it clearing away any negative thoughts in your mind and opening you up to a vast well of creativity and inspiration.

You are a freedom thinker, no idea is too big or too small.

This is your mind.

What would you do if you knew you could not fail?

Allow the image to come to your mind. See it, feel it as you continue to concentrate and breathe.

As the light softly expands beyond your head you see your home - lit up in this golden light - what would you do for your family if you knew you couldn't fail?

See it and feel it with each breath.

Allow the image to settle as the light continues to expand beyond your home and opens up to cover the entire planet. One person can change the world.

See the planet bathed in the light of your creative inspiration and see the image unfold in your mind - what would you do for the planet if you knew you could not fail?

Breathe it in. Allow the image to settle and you feel the light returning to your body and slowly when you are ready, open your eyes and come back to the feeling of your material body.

73

Hidden depth

"Everything is energy and
that's all there is to it."

Albert Einstein

date:

today in my world...

i am grateful for:

Beneath our skin we are all very similar.

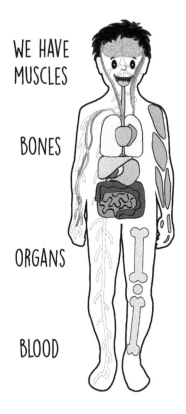

WE HAVE MUSCLES

BONES

ORGANS

BLOOD

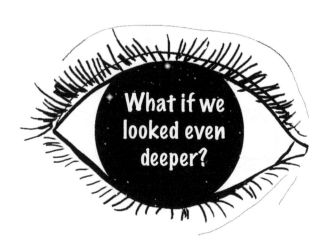

What if we looked even deeper?

we find cells that make up our tissue

deeper still we find atoms

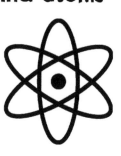

Atoms are 99.999% 'empty space'

Only .001% is actually solid. That part is called the nucleus.

We are made up of billions and billions and billions of atoms

PUT TOGETHER ALL THE SOLID MASS AND YOU ARE AS BIG AS A PIECE OF DUST.

that means we are 99.999% empty space

but what does that mean?

What is happening inside this empty space really?

movement

lots of it

MOVEMENT IS ENERGY

so that 99.999% empty space is ...

energy

Energy moves in waves

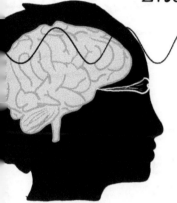

SOME ENERGY WE CAN SEE WITH OUR EYES, LIKE LIGHT

Think about dropping a pebble into a very still pond.

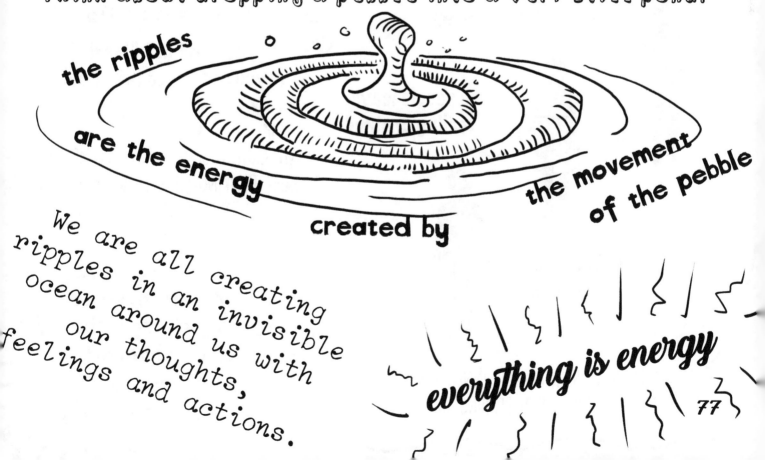

the ripples

are the energy

created by

the movement of the pebble

We are all creating ripples in an invisible ocean around us with our thoughts, feelings and actions.

everything is energy

77

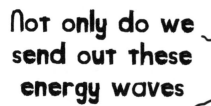

Not only do we send out these energy waves

we also receive them.

remember – we are 99.999% empty space

We are like little radio or wifi towers, sending and receiving signals with each other.

A bit like data sharing on phones

SO ENERGY CAN EASILY PASS THROUGH US JUST LIKE A RIPPLE ON A POND.

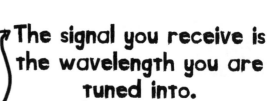

The signal you receive is the wavelength you are tuned into.

Exactly like a radio

you can't get Classic FM if you are tuned into Rock FM!

"WE CANNOT SOLVE OUR PROBLEMS WITH THE SAME THINKING WE USED WHEN WE CREATED THEM." ALBERT EINSTEIN

We have to change the channel!

some people have a very calming energy

some people leave you feeling drained

some people's energy might make you feel uncomfortable

THE MORE IN TUNE WITH YOUR INNER SENSES YOU BECOME, THE BETTER YOU WILL BE AT READING THE ENERGY OF OTHERS.

CHOOSING THE ENERGY YOU WANT TO FOCUS ON IS LIKE SETTING YOUR INTENTION OR WRITING YOUR AUTO—SUGGESTION.

You have been doing it throughout the journal with the gratitude focus each week.

i am grateful for.

Yes, your energy will change

and emotions can come and go like the weather.

Remember, your mind is a garden.

WHAT YOU FOCUS ON EXAPNDS

and you can change how you are feeling by changing your focus.

So keep tuning into the energy you want to feel.

EVEN WHEN THE 'SIGNAL' GETS WEAK OR YOU LOSE IT COMPLETELY.

Don't just listen to radio static, tune the radio, or change the channel.

tune yourself back in.

What is your network called?

HINT: THIS IS SIMILAR TO YOUR INTENTION. IT'S THE FEELING YOU WANT TO FOCUS ON

How do you feel when you have a clear signal?

What makes the signal weak?

How do you strengthen your signal?

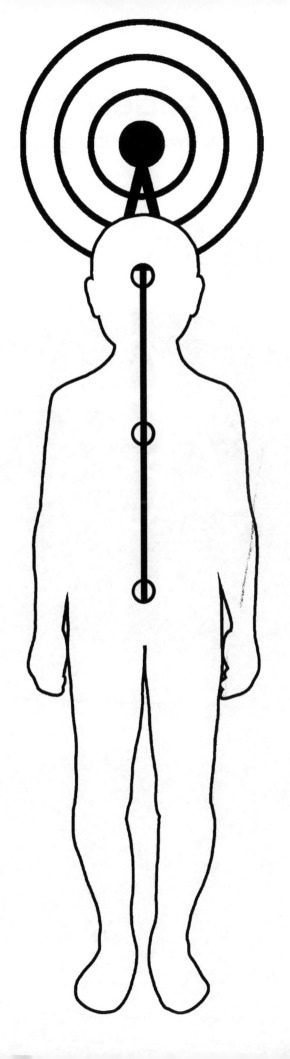

let's do a guided meditation

www.mywellbeingschool.com/universe9

Tuning In

Scan me

Tune In

Close your eyes and relax,

Take some deep conscious breaths.

With every breath you take, feel your mind calming down, your emotions settling as you connect to the Life inside you.

Start by focusing on your skin.
Feel as you continue to breathe how the surface of your skin feels, as though it expands as you breathe in, contracting as you breathe out.

Feel your skin, breathing. Feel the air entering into the soles of your feet. Can you feel it?

As you continue to concentrate on your soft rhythmic breathing, allow yourself to enter deeper inside your body, and feel your muscles. Feel the external muscles, relaxing more with each breath you take. Slowly you enter deeper into the small muscles surrounding your joints and your spine. Enter deeper still into your blood, pumped through your body by your heart, charged with the clean air you pull inside your body with each breath.

Feel the air as it enters your body, the beats of your heart, the rhythm of your breath.

The life inside you. The energy in each cell, sustaining you each moment.

Breathe deeply and give thanks to this life inside you, now think about the energy you want to spread into the world.

Feel it inside you, strengthening with each beat of your heart. Feel it inside your blood, your bones, your muscles, your skin.

Be the energy you want in your life.

Hold the feeling for as long as you like.

And when you are ready, come back to the feeling of your material body and bring this feeling with you for the rest of the week.

Grow with the flow

"I am rooted but I flow."

Virginia Woolf

Have you ever had the feeling that you can do literally anything?

↝ You feel happy,

✓ focused,

☆ *powerful*, AND EVERYTHING JUST FLOWS EASILY.

Have you had one of those days when you feel that you just can't do anything well and everything keeps going wrong?

Have you ever woken up one day and just felt generally grumpy or angry for no real reason?

⤷ or worried and anxious?

These are all **different 'states'** that we can get into.

THINK ABOUT 'STATE' AS THE ENERGY YOU ARE CARRYING AROUND. THE NETWORK YOU ARE TUNED INTO.

thoughts create feelings → **our body responds to these thoughts and feelings** → **puts us into a state** →

How would you sit if you were bored?

How would you sit if you were listening to the most interesting thing you ever heard?

Your body and mind are in a constant two way communication.

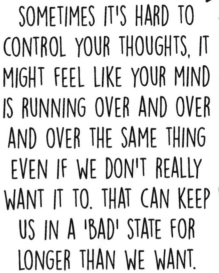

Sending and receiving information through the central nervous system in your spine.

SOMETIMES IT'S HARD TO CONTROL YOUR THOUGHTS, IT MIGHT FEEL LIKE YOUR MIND IS RUNNING OVER AND OVER AND OVER THE SAME THING EVEN IF WE DON'T REALLY WANT IT TO. THAT CAN KEEP US IN A 'BAD' STATE FOR LONGER THAN WE WANT.

did you know you can hack your mind with your body?

Stress or worry about something that is going to happen or that has happened is often a cause for keeping us in a negative state.

we can go from feeling like this

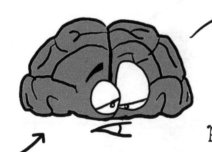

into this with a simple physical trigger

You might have seen professional athletes getting into the 'zone' before a competition.

THE WAY A TENNIS PLAYER BOUNCES THE BALL IN EXACTLY THE SAME WAY BEFORE EACH SERVE HELPS THEM TO FOCUS THE MIND THROUGH A PHYSICAL TRIGGER.

What would you say the strongest shape is? Draw it there

Did you draw a triangle? Or a circle?

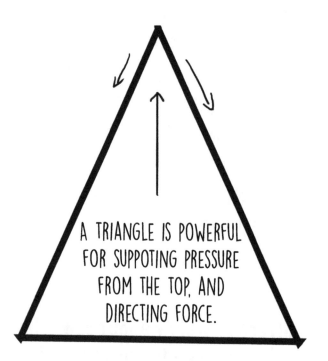

A TRIANGLE IS POWERFUL FOR SUPPOTING PRESSURE FROM THE TOP, AND DIRECTING FORCE.

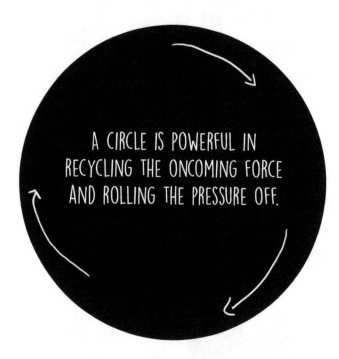

A CIRCLE IS POWERFUL IN RECYCLING THE ONCOMING FORCE AND ROLLING THE PRESSURE OFF.

Both shapes are very powerful in their own way.

The triangle is our focus

The circle is the state we create for ourself

focus creates state

state creates focus

HOW DO WE BREAK THE CYCLE WHEN WE FEEL IN A NEGATIVE STATE?

ANOTHER WAY TO SAY WHAT WE FOCUS ON EXPANDS.

focus creates state - State creates focus

88 SO WHAT STATE DO YOU WANT AND HOW CAN YOU CHANGE IT WHEN YOU NEED TO?

"Water is the driving force of all nature."
Leonardo Da Vinci, Polymath

"Be like water making its way through cracks. Do not be assertive, but adjust to the object, and you shall find a way around or through it. If nothing within you stays rigid, outward things will disclose themselves.

Empty your mind, be formless. Shapeless, like water. If you put water into a cup, it becomes the cup. You put water into a bottle and it becomes the bottle. You put it in a teapot, it becomes the teapot. Now, water can flow or it can crash. Be water, my friend." Bruce Lee, Kung Fu Legend

flow is the most powerful state to train.

OUR BODY IS ABOUT 80% WATER

THE POWER OF WATER COMES FROM ITS ABILTY TO ADAPT TO ANY ENVIRONMENT.

IF WE STAY CENTRED IN OURSELF, ANCHORED TO WHO WE ARE, THE FLOW WILL BECOME EFFORTLESS

flow state is connecting to the power and adaptability of water whilst staying centred and present in yourself.

We can't force things outside us to change, but we can flow through the storm with more stabilty and maybe even enjoy the ride.

Tools to change your state

explore what works best for you.

YOU JUST NEED TO FIND ONE THING THAT WORKS FOR YOU AND RUN WITH IT.

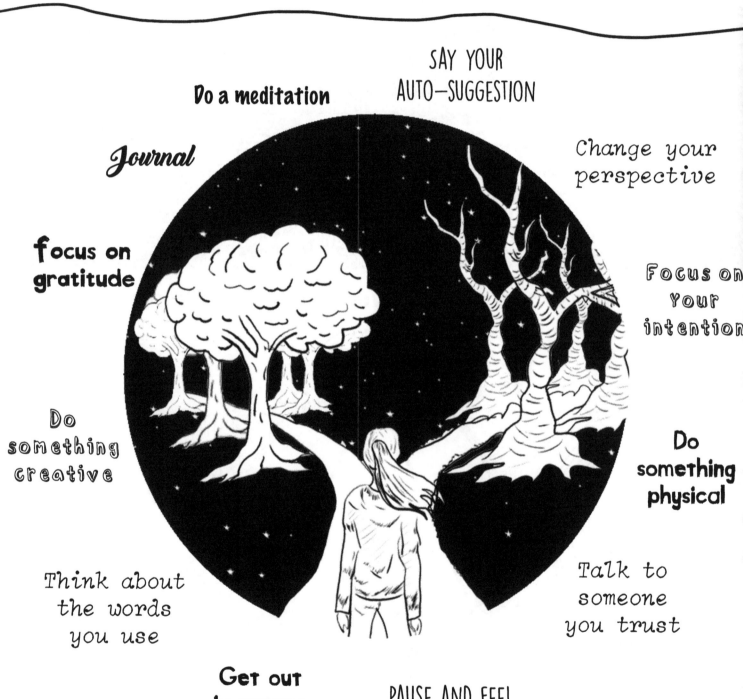

Do a meditation

SAY YOUR AUTO-SUGGESTION

Journal

Change your perspective

focus on gratitude

Focus on Your intention

Do something creative

Do something physical

Think about the words you use

Talk to someone you trust

Get out in nature

PAUSE AND FEEL YOUR CENTRE

"May your choices reflect your hopes not your fears."
Nelson Mandela

My flow State

I AM THINKING: I AM FEELING: I AM DOING:

my trigger to get into flow is:

let's do a guided meditation

www.mywellbeingschool.com/universe10

Find Your Flow

Scan me

Feel Your Flow

Close your eyes and take some deep comfortable breaths.

Feel the beats of your heart as you connect to the life inside you. As you feel the air entering inside your body, flowing through to every cell and atom of your being you feel your mind and emotions settle.

Now bring your awareness to the soles of both your feet. Feel being completely in the soles of your feet and imagine you have roots growing from your feet deep into the earth. Grounding you, connecting you to stability and balance.

These roots are bright and radiant and draw on the energy and vitality of the planet.

As you bring your awareness slowly up into your belly - you feel and see a tiny sky blue ball of light. This sky blue light instantly expands and washes through your entire body, filling you with the calming, peaceful light.

Connect to the element of water inside you, feel it calming you, relaxing, flowing through you.

Slowly allow your awareness to travel up into your chest. You see a tiny rosy flame kindled inside your heart. Focus on the feeling of love as you breathe deeply and feel the beats of your heart. Every beat of your heart is the universe whispering, 'I love you, I support you'.

Now feel this light expand to cover your entire body, the rosy light flowing through you, enriching your blood. Give thanks to this life.

Now move up into your head, and feel a golden light spread in and around your entire head centre. This light spreads and expands, filling your body and mind with your highest intention.

Breathe in these life-giving lights, as you feel the energy inside you expanding, opening up, creating a protective shield of light around your entire body. This bright white shield of light is your space, your energy, you control what happens, how you respond to the world outside.

Breathe in the power, the love, the courage, the inspiration to be yourself. Hold that space and now slowly, as you come back to the feeling of your material body, bring this feeling with you for the rest of the day.

date:

**One big idea i am
taking away with me is:**

this journal made me feel...

IT'S NOT ABOUT THE ANSWERS BUT THE QUESTIONS WE ASK THAT OPEN US TO THE SPECTRUM OF LIGHT THAT WAS ONCE INVISIBLE.

References

Brundtland, G. (1987) Our Common Future: The World Commission on Environment and Development. Oxford: Oxford University Press.

Davis, J. M. (2014). Examining early childhood education through the lens of education for sustainability: Revisioning rights. In J. Davis & S. Elliott (Eds.), Research in early childhood education for sustainability: International perspectives and provocations. pp. 21–37. London: Routledge.

Deleuze, G. & Guatarri, F. (1987). A Thousand Plateaus: Capitalism and schizophrenia. London: University of Minnesota Press.

Deleuze, G. (1995) Negotiations: 1972-1990. New York: Columbia University Press.

Hunter, M. A. Aprill, A. Hill, A and Emery, S. (2018) Education, Arts and Sustainability: Emerging Practice for a Changing World. Springer Briefs in Education.
Available at https://www.springer.com/gb/book/9789811077081 [Accessed August 2020]

Jickling, B. and Wals,J. (2008) Globalisation and environmental education; looking beyond sustainable development. Curriculum Studies, Vol 40. No 1. Pp1-21.

Sudhir, A. & Sen, A. (2000) Human Development and Economic Sustainability World Development. Vol 28, No 12, pp 2029-2049.

Tillmanns, T. (2017). "Disruptive Learning: Re-orientating Frames of Mind Towards Becoming Sustainability Change Agents." PhD thesis, Dublin City University

UNESCO (2015) Transforming our World: the 2030 Agenda for Sustainable Development.
Available from https://sustainabledevelopment.un.org/post2015/transformingourworld [Accessed August 2020]

Sources of Inspiration

Atteshlis, Stylianos (1998). The Symbol of Life. Cyprus: The Stoa Series.

Bogduk, Nikolai (2005). Clinical Anatomy of the Lumbar Spine and Sacrum. Elsevier Churchill Livingstone.

Brown, Brené (2015). Rising Strong. London: Vermilion.

Campbell, Joseph (1990). The Hero's Journey, Joseph Campbell on his life and work. California: New York Library.

Calais-Germain, Blandine (1993). Anatomy of Movement. Seattle: Eastland Press.

Clark, Alison (2017). Listening To Young Children; A guide to understanding and using the mosaic approach. Third Edition, London: Jessica Kingsley Publishers.

Davis, J. M. (2014). Examining early childhood education through the lens of education for sustainability: Revisioning rights. In J. Davis & S. Elliott (Eds.), Research in early childhood education for sustainability: International perspectives and provocations. London: Routledge.

Dispenza, Joe (2017). Becoming Supernatural. Hay House Inc.

Dweck, Carol (2006). Mindset; Changing the way you think to fulfil your potential. New York: Random House.

Eden, Donna and Feinstein, David (1998). Energy Medicine; Balancing your body's energies for optimal health, joy and vitality. New York: Jeremy P. Tarcher / Penguin.

Freire, Paulo (1970). Pedagogy Of The Oppressed. New York: Continuum.

Galfard, Christophe (2016). The Universe in Your Hand; A Journey Through Space, Time, and Beyond. New York: Flatiron Books.

Hawkins, David R (2009). Healing and Recovery. Sedona: Veritas.

James, Alice and Stowell, Louie, (2018). Looking After Your Mental Health. London: Usborne.

Mandela, Nelson (1965). No Easy Walk To Freedom. UK: Heinemann Educational Publishers.

Plato, edited by Cooper, John M (1997). Plato Complete Works. USA: Hackett Publishing.

Robinson, Ken and Aronica, Lou (2015). Creative Schools: The Grassroots Revolution That's Transforming Education. UK: Penguin

Siegel, Daniel J. and Bryson, Tina Payne (2012). The Whole-Brain Child: 12 Revolutionary Strategies to Nurture Your Child's Developing Mind. Melbourne: Scribe.

Wordsworth, William (1807) .Poems, in Two Volumes. London: Longman, Hurst, Rees, and Orme.

Other titles by H. J. Ray
inspiring self-awareness

ROBIN'S SWEET HEARTBEAT
A story about connection

MY BARE FEET
A little book filled with heart
for grounding and mindfulness

About the Author

Author of Robin's Sweet Heartbeat, My Bare Feet, and founder of My Wellbeing School, H. J. Ray's work inspires self-reflection through open-ended learning resources on wellbeing and mindfulness.

Trained at the Royal Central School of Speech and Drama in applied theatre and education, coupled with over a decade teaching meditation and wellbeing, in Hong Kong, Cyprus and now Australia, Heather offers a dynamic and heuristic approach wellbeing.

www.mywellbeingschool.com
@mywellbeingschool